DRONE OPERATORS

What It Takes to Join the Elite

TIM RIPLEY

Cavendish Square

New York

Published in 2016 by Cavendish Square Publishing, LLC
243 5th Avenue, Suite 136, New York, NY 10016

© 2016 Brown Bear Books Ltd

First Edition

Website: cavendishsq.com

CPSIA Compliance Information: Batch #WS15CSQ

Library of Congress Cataloging-in-Publication Data

Ripley, Tim.
 Drone operators : what it takes to join the elite / Tim Ripley.
    pages cm. — (Military jobs)
 Includes bibliographical references and index.
 ISBN 978-1-50260-520-7 (hardcover) ISBN 978-1-50260-521-4 (ebook)
 1. Drone aircraft. 2. Air pilots, Military—United States 3. United States—Armed Forces—Vocational guidance. I. Title.

 UG1242.D7R57 2015
 358.4—dc23

                        2015004967

For Brown Bear Books Ltd:
Editorial Director: Lindsey Lowe
Managing Editor: Tim Cooke
Children's Publisher: Anne O'Daly
Design Manager: Keith Davis
Designer: Lynne Lennon
Picture Manager: Sophie Mortimer

Picture Credits:
T=Top, C=Center, B=Bottom, L=Left, R=Right

Front Cover: U.S. Department of Defense
All images U.S. Department of Defense except: Boeing Integrated Defense Systems: 45; General Atomics Aeronautical Systems: 44; Getty Images: Crown Copyright 41; Library of Congress: 7; Northrop Grumman Corporation: 23; Robert Hunt Library: 38, 43.
Artistic Effects: Shutterstock

Brown Bear Books has made every attempt to contact the copyright holder.
If you have any information please contact licensing@brownbearbooks.co.uk

We believe the extracts included in this book to be material in the public domain.
Anyone having any further information should contact licensing@brownbearbooks.co.uk

Manufactured in the United States of America

CONTENTS

INTRODUCTION

In little over twenty years, unmanned aerial vehicles (UAVs)—popularly known as drones—have changed the face of warfare. The men and women who operate them are pioneers with their own special skill set.

All arms of the military now use drones of various sizes. Some are used for surveillance. Others are armed with missiles and bombs to strike at targets. The US military now has more than seven thousand drones. In the last decade they have been used in conflicts in Afghanistan, Iraq, Libya, and Syria.

Drones are flown remotely via video links. Many people compare operating a drone to playing a video game. Drone operators know, however, that there is one big difference: drones cause real damage and kill real people. Operators work in teams. Pilots steer the aircraft, while sensor operators direct their cameras and radar. Image analysts pore over the intelligence the drones gather. On air bases around the world, forward operators and technicians keep drones flying over potential trouble spots.

 Technicians on a base in Iraq fit a Targeting System Ball to a Predator. The ball contains sensing equipment.

⯈⯈ HISTORY

The US military first experimented with unmanned aerial vehicles in the 1950s. During the Vietnam War (1965–1975), US Air Force drones took reconnaissance photographs of enemy territory.

This early version of the RQ-1 Predator was photographed in 1995, when the aircraft was used for reconnaissance.

The US military has remained at the forefront of using unmanned military technology. Development began relatively slowly, however. It was only in 1994 that early drones—called the Predator air vehicle—were first used in military operations. Seven years later, the Predator was modified to fire Hellfire guided missiles. It fired them in action for the first time in Afghanistan in 2001.

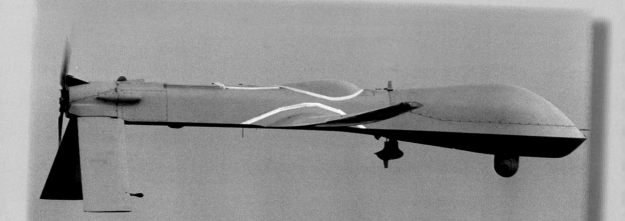

 During the Vietnam War, drones took aerial images like this one of a US military base.

Drones in Action

Every branch of the US military now uses unmanned air systems. The Marines fly them off the decks of warships, while army infantry patrols carry small versions in their backpacks. The Air Force has giant, unmanned strategic spy aircraft and the Navy catapults drones off aircraft carriers.

US unmanned air vehicles have seen action in conflict zones around the world from the Balkans to Africa, Iraq, and Afghanistan. They have helped law enforcement agencies monitor America's borders and have also assisted in assessing the extent of natural disasters at home and abroad.

IN ACTION

Drones remain controversial. Drone attacks in Pakistan and Afghanistan have killed a number of civilians, including children. Critics say this breaks the rules of war. The US military argues that drones actually reduce the chance of accidental deaths because they pinpoint targets so precisely.

WHAT IT TAKES

"Piloting" a drone is not like flying a conventional aircraft. Not every pilot can make the transition to unmanned aircraft. Controlling an airplane remotely requires different thought processes.

The key skill is "spatial awareness." Pilots in aircraft use their eyes and ears to understand what is happening around them. Their brains react rapidly to visual and audio input. Drone operators work with only a limited view from the air vehicle's camera, together with data from instruments

 Technicians check the systems of a Reaper drone before a mission.

giving the craft's height, altitude, direction, and speed. The operator might also have radar showing the position of nearby aircraft.

Building a Picture

Drone pilots have to instantly use this data to build a three-dimensional image of the aircraft's location in their minds. Doing this without being onboard requires unique skills. Some drone pilots liken it to an "out-of-body experience." They have to use the data to imagine themselves in a situation hundreds of miles away.

 A Reaper crew from the 91st Attack Squadron flies a drone mission in 2014. A drone crew includes a pilot, a sensor operator, and an analyst.

EYEWITNESS

"I couldn't tell which way it was turning, or if it was straight, if it was upside down, or if it was right-side up ... I couldn't grasp what was happening with the aircraft."

—Unnamed drone operator on becoming disoriented

⟫ TRAINING CENTER

Deep in the Nevada desert is a remote airfield that has become the hub of US drone operations. This is Creech Air Force Base (Creech AFB), which was first created to train air gun crews in World War II.

Today, the air above the desert is full of the low whine of Predator and Reaper engines around the clock. The drones fly training missions over a huge range outside Las Vegas.

A pilot (back) and sensor operator (forefront) follow a vehicle with a drone during an exercise.

 A drone operator (center) briefs maintenance and avionics specialists on a mission.

Creech Air Force Base

Creech AFB is the home of the 432nd Wing, which oversees all US Air Force drone operations. There is so much demand for trained personnel that the Air Force has also set up several training outstations. Instructors at Creech developed training courses to meet the surge in demand for crews—both air and ground—after the start of the war in Afghanistan in 2001. Creech is also the hub of America's global drone operations. Hundreds of air crew and intelligence analysts serve there. They are able to pass on lessons from the front line to new generations of operators.

EYEWITNESS

"You're absolutely there, you're in the fight. You're hearing the guys on the ground and you're hearing their stress, so when you finish your shift it's very odd to then step outside ... It's the middle of the day and you're in Las Vegas."

—Paul Rolfe, former drone operator

▶▶ PILOT TRAINING

The operators of the earliest drones were experienced fighter pilots. Today, demand for drone operators is so high that this is no longer possible. All drone operators have to be able to fly an airplane, however.

Drone operators use video images and maps to chart the progress of their aircraft during a mission.

Unlike traditional US Air Force flying training courses, learning to fly drones takes place mainly in classrooms. Some candidates are experienced pilots, but others have no actual flying experience.

 Trainee drone operators fly DA-20 trainer aircraft during flight screening. Only successful candidates will progress.

They enter drone training direct from the US Air Force Academy or from officer training units.

Flight Training

These new students undergo forty hours of initial flight screening in a Diamond DA-20 trainer aircraft. This gives them basic flying skills and a sense of spatial awareness in the air. About a quarter of students fail this stage of training. Successful candidates go to Randolph Air Force Base in Texas. They spend two to three months flying by instruments alone in a

Beechcraft T-6 Texan II simulator. The candidates then spend three months at a readiness training unit flying unmanned aircraft. This includes 15.5 hours of academic time, nine simulator sessions totaling 22.5 hours, and seven flights totaling 14 hours.

EYEWITNESS

"You need classic pilot training to fly a drone. Absolutely. We have a stick, we have a rudder; you're flying an airplane, you're just doing it remotely. All the same skills are necessary. You have to worry about the traditional things that concern pilots."

—Daniel Rothenberg, former drone pilot

▶▶ IMAGE ANALYSIS

Intelligence and image analysts are key to the success of drone missions. They tell the pilots exactly what the pilots are looking at and where to strike.

Drone control cabins contain not only the pilot's station but also computer screens where analysts view real-time video imagery being collected by the drone's sensors. Analysts have extensive training in examining the imagery. They are looking for suspicious activity or trying to identify enemy equipment or bases.

 This video image of a truck taken from the sensor of a Reaper drone contains targeting information for the drone operators.

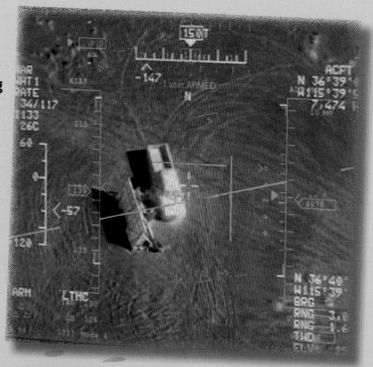

Reading an Image

The analysts can zoom in on details in a picture. They can also call up databases of imagery from previous missions to look for changes in terrain or buildings. With high-quality images, they can compare individuals on the screen with pictures of known enemy leaders.

Analysts use secure Internet connections to coordinate with eavesdropping organizations or other drone crews to hunt for specific targets. This allows drone operations to work efficiently with other intelligence agencies.

 Technicians from the 432nd Aircraft Communications Maintenance Squadron check details of a ground control station at Creech Air Force Base.

EYEWITNESS

"I don't have any video games that ask me to sit in one seat for six hours and look at the same target. One of the things we beat into our crews is that this is a real aircraft, and whatever decisions you make, there's going to be consequences."

—Sensor operator trainer, Holloman AFB

FORWARD AIR CONTROL

In situations where drones operate near civilian centers or friendly forces, observers on the scene can help ensure a drone target is identified correctly. This is the job of forward air controllers.

 A forward air controller calls in the position of his unit.

In such sensitive situations, forward air controllers (or joint terminal attack controllers) help drone operators identify friendly targets from hostile targets. This is more reliable than people looking at a screen.

On the Ground

Forward controllers use covert insertion techniques to get as close to a target as possible. They use satellite radios to talk to the drone crew. They make sure that everyone involved in the action is looking at the same thing. They do this by streaming video from the drone direct to a laptop-sized remotely operated video receiver (ROVER) terminal carried in their packs. They use pre-arranged steps, or protocols, to guide an air strike.

Drone crews and ground controllers have intensive training in air-support protocols. This culminates in live fire exercises in the Nevada Desert. Drone crews drop real bombs under the direction of ground controllers.

IN ACTION

Forward air controllers are one of the US Air Force's main weapons in trying to avoid accidental casualties from drone strikes. They can remain in place close to a potential target for days, communicating with the drone operators. Together, they help make a definite identification of a target and work out the safest time to strike.

▶▶ A forward air controller coordinates air cover in the Sroghar Mountains of Afghanistan in 2004.

DRONE PILOT

The job of a US Air Force drone operator is essentially the same as that of a pilot: to fly an aircraft on a mission. The only difference is that these pilots are nowhere near their aircraft.

The pilot actually controls or "flies" the drone on its mission. As with a conventional pilot, he or she is also the commander of the mission. The commander is responsible for coordinating the various personnel and agencies involved.

 A drone operator controls his aircraft as he talks to his crew by radio.

Commander's Role

A mission begins with a briefing. The launch and recovery team joins the briefing via the Internet. When the mission begins, the pilot steers the drone to the area of operations. He or she then sets it up to circle possible targets. In coordination with sensor operators and image analysts, the pilot positions the drone to get the best view to identify a target.

Once controllers have positively identified a target, it is the pilot's job to confirm it as a valid target. He or she then presses the weapon release button.

 Predator operators pilot separate drones on missions to support Operation Iraqi Freedom from a ground control station on Balad Air Base, Iraq, in July 2004.

EYEWITNESS

"Drones allow operators to be much more calm, cool, and collected. They allow people to have a discussion about whether a target is the right target or not. There is no question in my mind that drone warfare is much better and safer."

—Mary Cummings, former US Navy fighter pilot

SENSORS AND INTELLIGENCE

The more analysts study the images from a drone, the more chance there is that they will interpret the pictures accurately. As many analysts as possible watch video imagery as it comes in from the drone.

Sensor operators control the drone's video cameras and synthetic aperture radar, which generates two-dimensional radar images. They ensure that the sensors have continuous coverage to capture the best images of intended targets.

 Air Force analysts work in a facility for intelligence, surveillance, and reconnaissance.

UNCLASSIFIED

HA
DOI: 23JAN10
GEO: 183307N0722041W

= PASSABLE ROAD

This drone image shows Haiti after an earthquake in 2010. Analysts have marked closed and open roads to help the military relief mission.

Analyzing Intelligence

The sensor operator monitors imagery from the drone for targets that might need to be engaged. Moving targets can be tracked by initiating the sensor's computerized auto-lock. In back of the control cabin, image analysts conduct a painstaking examination of the imagery. The analysts operate in shifts as they pore over video footage, looking for targets. They use advanced software to study terrain or buildings to identify enemy positions.

EYEWITNESS

"At 5,000 feet, I could tell you what type of clothes a person is wearing and if they have a beard, their hair color ... If someone sits down on a cold surface for a while and then gets up, you'll see the heat from the person for a long time. It kinda looks like a white blossom ... It's quite beautiful."

—Unnamed drone sensor operator

▶▶ LAUNCH AND RECOVERY

Drones are launched as close to their targets as possible. Small detachments of personnel known as Launch and Recovery Elements (LRE) are positioned in combat zones to launch and retrieve drones.

 A US Marine in Afghanistan recovers an RQ-7B Shadow drone after a mission.

These specialist teams refuel, service, and rearm drones at forward airstrips. They use equipment flown in on C-130 Hercules airlifters.

A small command team receives a daily flight program of launches from the control center. The program lists targets to be monitored and any weapons loads.

 A Bat 12 stealth drone is shot into the sky from a mobile launcher that can be towed behind a truck.

Flying the Mission

A pilot at the forward airstrip receives clearance from air traffic control and launches the drone. He takes the aircraft up to its cruising altitude then hands over to a control center in the United States. At the end of a mission, control is handed back to the forward-based pilot, who brings the drone back in to land.

EYEWITNESS

"The launching and landing of the plane is the best part. You hook it up to a bungee cord, stretch it out, and let it go. After it goes over fifty feet per second, the motor engages. After that, it flies itself on the path you have programmed."

—Nancy Gonzalez, drone launch team, Afghanistan

23

>> COMPUTER PROGRAMMING

The US Air Force drone program depends on reliable computer systems. This specialist support is provided by civilian contractors. Civilian specialists have been heavily involved in drone operations since the start of the program.

Civilian contractors from engineering firms involved in building drones often send technicians to war zones in order to troubleshoot technical glitches. During highly classified missions where military personnel cannot take part, civilian contractors might be asked to set up drone launch and recovery elements at airstrips near battle zones.

 Senior Airman Zachariah Grummons works on an Air Force database in Montgomery, Alabama.

Large drones are controlled by software programs that are regularly upgraded, so computer programmers are often sent to forward locations. This is an unusual role for experts more used to working in offices.

 A technician works in the server room of the Defense Information Systems Agency at Tinker Air Force Base in Oklahoma.

Control Centers

At drone control centers in the United States, contractors set up and maintain databases to manage video imagery and other intelligence collected by drones. These databases are connected across secure Internet links. No security breach can be permitted.

IN ACTION

One of the major issues facing computer experts in military intelligence is data storage. High-resolution images and video footage use a huge amount of computer memory, so military servers are continually being filled. One answer is to store this intelligence in the Cloud, but that would only be possible if experts are sure that they can make it impossible for hackers to access it.

HANDHELD DRONE TEAMS

Frontline combat units routinely use handheld drones as their "eyes in the sky." These small drones resemble remote-control modern aircraft. They are operated by two-man teams.

Handheld drone teams live with combat units so they can be ready whenever necessary. They can unpack and assemble a drone in minutes.

A Special Forces operator launches a handheld Raven drone into the air at a base in California.

In the Air

One soldier launches the aircraft by starting the petrol engine and throwing the drone into the sky. The operator then takes over with a laptop computer configured to operate as a control console. The operator uses a live video feed to look for hostile activity on the ground. This allows him to warn commanders of any ground troops in the area of enemy threats. By pinpointing the location of any hostile forces, he can coordinate fire support from artillery or aircraft.

A mini drone is assembled from its carrying cases. The aircraft can fly for about an hour.

EYEWITNESS

"The on-the-ground team do their own work on the bird [drone] if it breaks. They put the pieces back together and use glue or tape: whatever it takes to keep it flying. They do all the maintenance."

—Chief Master Sergeant Nicholas Liberti, Operations Superintendent, Edwards AFB

⟫ MQ-1 PREDATOR

The Predator is the key drone associated with the "War on Terrorism." Early versions were developed by the Californian company General Atomics in the 1990s and saw service over Bosnia and Kosovo.

 Senior Airman Valerie Santa checks the oil level in the engine of a Predator at a US base in Iraq.

The Predator is a medium-altitude long-endurance (MALE) drone. It has a range of up to 770 miles (1,239 km) and can stay in the air over targets for up to twenty-four hours. But the Predator's piston engine is not very powerful. It has a top speed of only 135 miles per hour (217 kmh).

 The Predator's Hellfire missiles are carried on hardpoints in the middle of the aircraft.

Sensors and Satellites

The Predator's thermal-imaging camera is in a sensor ball just below its nose. It can monitor targets 25,000 feet (7,620 m) below. No one on the ground can hear or see the circling Predator. Above the nose, a satellite dish enclosed in a dome streams video to control centers in the United States. By 2000, Predators were fitted with two Hellfire missiles. They were used during the US invasion of Afghanistan in 2001.

MQ-1 PREDATOR
Top speed: 135 mph (217 kmh)
Range: 770 miles (1,239 km)
Length: 27 feet (8.22 m)
Wingspan: 55 feet (16.8 m)
Weapons: 2 x AGM-114 Hellfire missiles

EYEWITNESS

"Perhaps the Predator's best quality is that it can spend some twenty-four hours in the air, flying at heights of up to twenty-six thousand feet."

—P W Singer, Strategist, New American Foundation

MQ-9 REAPER

The Reaper is a bigger, more powerful version of the Predator. It was created by General Atomics in order to expand the range, endurance, and power of the US Air Force drone fleet.

The Predator could only carry two Hellfire missiles. This prevented drones from making multiple strikes on a target. The arrival of the Reaper in 2007 overcame this limitation. The Reaper flies twice as fast as a Predator and can carry four Hellfire missiles and two 500-pound (227 kg) laser-guided bombs.

 Ground crews demonstrate how to fit a sensor camera to the underside of an MQ-9 Predator.

 Airmen at Creech Air Force Base prepare an MQ-9 Reaper for a flight during an exercise in May 2014.

Target Finding

The Reaper finds its targets with a thermal-imaging video camera. It also carries a synthetic aperture radar that creates two-dimensional radar images. The Reaper's ability to find targets in bad weather can be used by its GPS-guided missiles. Unlike its laser-guided bombs, they can be used to hit specific target coordinates without guidance. Lasers can be interrupted by rain, cloud, or fog.

MQ-9 REAPER
Top speed: 300 mph (482 kmh)
Range: 1,151 miles (1,852 km)
Length: 36 feet (11 m)
Wingspan: 66 feet (20 m)
Weapons: 4 x Hellfire missiles, 2 x laser-guided bombs

EYEWITNESS

"We've moved from using UAVs mainly in intelligence, surveillance, and reconnaissance roles before Operation Iraqi Freedom to a true hunter-killer role with the Reaper."

—T. Michael Moseley, Chief of Staff, US Air Force

RQ-4 GLOBAL HAWK

The biggest drone in service with the US Air Force is the RQ-4 Global Hawk. It is unarmed, but it can carry out surveillance operations anywhere in the world.

Technicians check a Global Hawk's engine. The bulge at the front of the aircraft holds its sensors.

The jet-powered Global Hawk has replaced a previous generation of high-altitude spy planes. It can remain airborne for over thirty hours. The Global Hawk is launched by a forward Launch and Recovery Element and flown by a Mission Control Element from a

 Ground crew pepare an RQ-4 Global Hawk for a mission at a base in Southwest Asia.

drone base. The aircraft flies on a pre-programmed course, but the crew can change the course at any time.

Sensors

The Global Hawk's sensors include wide-area cameras to photograph whole countries, or telescopic cameras to zoom in on specific locations. The moving-target indicator radar can track enemy vehicles or keep a whole army under surveillance. The radar is being modified by the US Navy to monitor naval operations at sea.

RQ-4 GLOBAL HAWK
Cruising speed: 375 mph (604 kmh)
Range: 14,155 miles (22,780 km)
Length: 47.6 feet (14.5 m)
Wingspan: 130.9 feet (39.9 m)
Weapons: none

EYEWITNESS

"If there's a sensor that's important, why not put it on Global Hawk and fly it for thirty hours? Flying over Afghanistan or Iraq or the Pacific or Japan during a tsunami, carrying sensors such a long distance for such a long time is crucial."

—Ed Walby, Northrop Grumann, RQ-4 manufacturer

⏵⏵ DESERT HAWK

The Lockheed Martin Desert Hawk is typical of the handheld drones used by the US military. It is carried in a travel case and can be assembled or disassembled in a matter of minutes.

The Desert Hawk weighs only 7 pounds (3.2 kg) and is launched by being thrown or fired into the air with a bungee cord. It can fly for up to an hour. The pilot sets a course past set points and can transmit new coordinates to the drone in the air if new

 A drone operator prepares to launch a Desert Hawk by hand in the Iraqi desert.

targets need to be investigated. The drone's three cameras transmit live pictures back to the control console, where they are recorded on a hard drive for analysis. The Desert Hawk is now being replaced by the RQ-11 Raven, which flies longer and farther than the older drone.

 A forward drone operator uses a handheld console to follow a Desert Hawk mission.

DESERT HAWK
Top speed: 55 mph (89 kmh)
Range: 9.3 miles (15 km)
Length: 32 inches (81 cm)
Wingspan: 52 inches (1.32 m)
Weapons: none

EYEWITNESS

"I don't steer the plane, but if I see something suspicious I can program it to go elsewhere. I can also have it hover overhead and move the camera to view."

—Nancy Gonzalez, drone launch team, Afghanistan

▷▷ X-47 CARRIER DRONE

During 2011, the US Navy and the engineering firm Northrop Grumman began to test if it was possible to operate drones from aircraft carriers.

In early trials, the X-47B drone was able to land on the deck of a Nimitz-class aircraft carrier. It could also be catapulted off the ship's deck into the air. In expanded trials, the X-47B shared the carrier deck with manned F/A-18 Hornet fighter jets.

 An X-47B takes off from the deck of a Nimitz-class aircraft carrier.

 An X-47B lands after a test flight. Carriers will likely carry both drones and piloted aircraft.

Further Development

The Navy plans further trials on other combat drones. The trials will discover if it is possible to carry out autonomous combat missions without any human pilots in the air or on the ground. The drone would be programmed to fly itself into enemy airspace and drop live weapons on targets. This would mean drones would not have to rely on vulnerable radio links to ground stations for instructions. The enemy would not be able to interfere with any radio signals.

X-47 CARRIER DRONE
Top speed: High subsonic
Range: 2,416 miles (3,889 km)
Length: 38.2 feet (11.6 m)
Wingspan: 62.1 feet (18.9 m)
Weapons: 4,500 lb (2,000 kg of ordnance)

IN ACTION

Landing drones on aircraft carriers is far more difficult than conventional drone operations on land. The moving deck of the ship means the drone pilot has to make constant adjustments as the aircraft descends. In addition, naval drones use special sensors to track targets at sea.

37

▶▶ AFGHANISTAN, 2001

On October 7, 2001, US airpower was unleashed against al-Qaeda terrorist bases in Afghanistan. Predator drones led the offensive, seeking out and targeting the most important targets.

In the opening hours of the US air offensive, operators used Predators to monitor a series of compounds where al-Qaeda and Taliban leaders were suspected to be hiding. As US bombs and missiles exploded around the cities of Kabul and Kandahar, the enemy leaders made their escape.

A Predator above Kandahar followed a convoy of vehicles suspected of carrying the Taliban leader Mullah Omar. It tracked him entering a mosque. There was a slight delay while the target was assessed. US commanders cleared US Navy FA-18 Hornet jets to drop laser-

Al-Qaeda leader Mohammed Atef was wanted for plotting the 9/11 attacks in 2000.

TALIBAN MILITARY BUILDINGS IN KABUL, AFGHANISTAN
POST STRIKE

guided bombs on the target, but the delay allowed Mullah Omar to escape in the confusion.

This aerial image shows damage from a drone attack on Kabul.

Terrorist Death

A month later, a drone spotted the al-Qaeda military chief Mohammed Atef fleeing from Kabul. Atef had planned the 9/11 terrorist attacks on the United States. A Predator drone tracked him to a compound in the city of Gardez. This time there was no delay. The Predator operator was cleared to engage the target and Atef was killed.

EYEWITNESS

"Often a drone operator has to track a subject for weeks beforehand. They aren't really like pilots, and they certainly aren't like artillerymen, where you never see the target. The better analogy is to snipers."

—Peter Asaro, School of Media Studies, New School, New York

BENGHAZI, LIBYA, 2011

In the spring of 2011, the Libyan ruler Muammar Gaddafi tried to crush a rebellion by his people against his dictatorial rule. Western countries provided an aerial shield to protect the rebels.

Airmen coordinate air operations onboard an E-3A Sentry aircraft.

The rebel stronghold in the city of Benghazi was under threat from Gaddafi's tanks and artillery. The rebels had few heavy weapons and no aircraft.

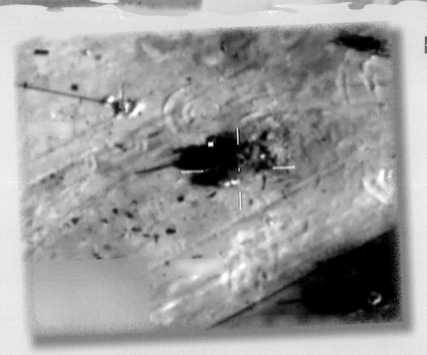

◄◄ Coalition missiles strike two Libyan army main battle tanks in the desert near the city of Benghazi.

International Force

British, Canadian, Danish, French, and Italian fighter bombers patrolled the desert to protect the rebels on the ground. US Air Force Predator drones located targets for the fighter planes. They picked out hidden tanks and artillery pieces.

Predator controllers at Creech Air Force Base in Nevada sent the coordinates of Libyan positions in coded chat room messages. The messages were picked up by a NATO E-3A Sentry AWACS (Airborne Warning and Control System) radar aircraft that was circling above the Mediterranean

Sea just off the Libyan coast. Controllers on the AWACS sent strike jets to hit the targets with laser-guided bombs and missiles. Operators kept the Predators overhead after the strike in order to assess the damage caused by the attacks.

EYEWITNESS

"Drones and robotic warfare are actually normal now. We've gone from using a handful of these systems to having around seven thousand in the air."

—P W Singer, Strategist, New American Foundation

ABBOTTABAD, PAKISTAN, 2011

On May 1, 2011, US Navy SEALs flew deep into Pakistan to raid a compound where the al-Qaeda chief Osama bin Laden was thought to be hiding. To ensure surprise, Washington did not warn Pakistan.

As part of the effort to avoid alerting the Pakistanis, US commanders used the top-secret Lockheed Martin RQ-170 Sentinel stealth drone. Its shape is designed to minimize the radar signals it reflects, so it is less likely to be detected by enemy radar. The RQ-170 flew alongside two Black Hawk MH-60 stealth helicopters that were carrying teams of US Navy SEALs. The SEALs would land inside the walls of the compound and storm the building in search of bin Laden.

This drone image of Abbottabad shows bin Laden's compound (outlined).

Vital Intelligence

Flying in Pakistani airspace, the Sentinel reached bin Laden's compound undetected. It began broadcasting video images. There was no sign that the al-Qaeda chief had been tipped off about the

 Drones allowed the mission planners to have a clear understanding of the layout of the compound behind the high walls.

planned raid. As the helicopters carrying the SEALs arrived, the drone continued to broadcast video imagery to the White House in Washington, DC. There, President Barack Obama, cabinet members, and senior military chiefs watched as the drama took place on the ground.

The Sentinel continued to circle overhead as the SEALs fought their way into the Abbottabad house and killed the al-Qaeda chief. As the SEALs left in their helicopters with bin Laden's body, the Sentinel's signals intelligence equipment monitored radio traffic to see if the Pakistanis had any idea of events as they unfolded. In fact, by the time the Pakistanis realized that anything was going on, the SEALs were long gone.

EYEWITNESS

"You have to step back and say, 'There's a reason these individuals were targeted.'"

—Unnamed drone operator, on killing targets

▶▶ FUTURE MISSIONS

Drone operators are set to become even more important in future wars. US military commanders are placing great emphasis on how the next generation of drones will be used in conflict.

Drones could be used for a wider range of missions. The missions might include patrolling oceans, attacking ships, or jamming enemy radio and Internet communications.

 The General Atomics Avenger made its initial test flight in 2009. It uses stealth technology to reduce its radar profile.

Drones might even engage enemy aircraft in air-to-air combat. New weapons will allow drones to strike a wider range of targets more accurately. This should help avoid collateral damage to nearby civilians.

 The X-45C is designed to replace conventional bombers.

Changing Roles

The role of drone operators will change, too. They may control drones from helicopters or aircraft in the air rather than from ground stations. They would create so-called "drone swarms" to subject the enemy to overwhelming attacks from multiple directions.

Autonomous drones, meanwhile, will be increasingly able to "think" for themselves. That will help them outmaneuver enemy drones that rely on radio links to ground control stations.

EYEWITNESS

"Drones will change war. What we will have ten years from now is going to make things that we are doing today seem almost primitive. What we call pilots today will change ... Maybe we won't even continue to call them pilots."
—Daniel Rothenberg, former drone operator

GLOSSARY

altitude The height above the ground at which an airplane flies.

autonomous Describes a device that controls itself.

avionics Electronic equipment fitted inside an aircraft.

bungee cord An elasticated band encased in a nylon sleeve.

Cloud A computer storage system that uses shared computing resources over the Internet.

collateral damage Accidental damage to something close to an intended target.

console A handset containing the controls for a device.

covert Something carried out in secret.

disoriented Having lost a sense of direction.

eavesdropping Secretly listening to communications.

guided missile A missile that can be steered toward its target.

hardpoints A bracket on an aircraft used to carry a load.

insurgents Rebels fighting against a government or an invasion force.

ordnance Weapons such as bombs, rockets, or missiles.

radar A system that uses radio waves to detect objects.

reconnaissance Observation of an enemy's position.

sensor Any device that detects and measures physical objects, buildings, or landscapes.

spatial awareness The knowledge of where one is in relation to surrounding objects.

stealth Technology used to disguise aircraft and vehicles to stop them being located by radar.

stick Short for joystick, the control column of an aircraft.

strategic Related to an overall or global scale.

surveillance Close observation of the enemy.

synthetic aperature radar A form of radar that generates two-dimensional images of terrain.

thermal-imaging camera A camera that detects heat, such as that given out by living creatures.

tsunami A destructive wave caused by an earthquake beneath the sea.

FURTHER INFORMATION

BOOKS

Collard, Sneed B. *Technology Forces: Drones and War Machines*. Freedom Forces. Vero Beach, FL: Rourke Educational Media, 2013.

Drones: From Insect Spy Drones to Bomber Drones. New York: Scholastic, 2014.

Hamilton, John. *UAVs: Unmanned Aerial Vehicles*. Xtreme Military Aircraft. Minneapolis, MN: Adbo & Daughters, 2012.

Masters, Nancy Robinson. *Drone Pilot*. Cool Military Careers. Ann Arbor, MI: Cherry Lake Publishing, 2012.

Nardo, Don. *Drones*. The Military Experience: In the Air. Greensboro, NC: Morgan Reynolds Publishing, 2013

Rose, Simon. *Drones*. Global Issues. New York: Av2 by Wiegl, 2014.

Wood, Alix. *Drone Operator*. The World's Coolest Jobs. New York: PowerKids Press, 2014.

WEBSITES

www.airforce.com/careers/detail/sensor-operator
US Air Force page about how to become a sensor operator.

www.creech.af.mil
Official website of Creech Air Force Base, home to most drone operators.

www.flyingmag.com/aircraft/drone-jobs-what-it-takes-fly-uav
An article on becoming a drone operator from *Flying* magazine.

militarycareers.about.com/od/Career-Profiles/p/Career-Profile-USAF-UAV-Operator.htm
A guide to careers for drone operators in the US Air Force.

Publisher's note to educators and parents: Our editors have carefully reviewed these websites to ensure that they are suitable for students. Many websites change frequently, however, and we cannot guarantee that a site's future contents will continue to meet our high standards of quality and educational value. Be advised that students should be closely supervised whenever they access the Internet.

INDEX